Hacking V

The Complete Beginner's Guide with Detailed Practical Examples of Wireless Networks Hacking & Penetration Testing To Fully Understand The Basics Of Computer Cyber Security

by

Learn Computer

Hacking In Deep

© Copyright 2019 by **_Learn Computer Hacking In Deep_**- All rights reserved.

This eBook is provided with the sole purpose of providing relevant information on a specific topic for which every reasonable effort has been made to ensure that it is both accurate and reasonable. Nevertheless, by purchasing this eBook you consent to the fact that the author, as well as the publisher, are in no way experts on the topics contained herein, regardless of any claims as such that may be made within. As such, any suggestions or recommendations that are made within are done so purely for entertainment value. It is recommended that you always consult a professional prior to undertaking any of the advice or techniques discussed within.

This is a legally binding declaration that is considered both valid and fair by both the Committee of Publishers Association and the American Bar Association and should be considered as legally binding within the United States.

The reproduction, transmission, and duplication of any of the content found herein, including any specific or extended information will be done as an illegal act regardless of the end from the information ultimately takes.

This includes copied versions of the work both physical, digital and audio unless express consent of the Publisher is provided beforehand. Any additional rights reserved.

Table of Contents

INTRODUCTION   4

HARD DRIVE INSTALLATION   23

WELL-SUITED PACKAGE HANDLING UTILITY   37

TARBALLS   47

A PRACTICAL GUIDE TO INSTALLING NESSUS   53

Introduction

Kali Linux is the world's generally well-known entrance testing stage, utilized by security experts in a wide scope of specializations. This includes infiltration testing, crime scene investigation, figuring out, and helplessness appraisal. It is the perfection of long stretches of refinement and the aftereffect of a persistent development of the stage, from WHoppiX to WHAX, to Back Track, and now to a total entrance testing structure utilizing numerous highlights of Debian GNU/Linux and the dynamic open source network around the world.

Kali Linux has not been created to be a basic assortment of devices, but instead an adaptable structure that expert infiltration analyzers, security aficionados, understudies, and novices can modify to accommodate their particular needs.

Why This Book?

Kali Linux isn't just an assortment of different data security apparatuses that are introduced on a standard Debian base and pre-arranged to get you going immediately. To capitalize on Kali, it is critical to have an intensive comprehension of its amazing Debian GNU/Linux underpinnings (which bolster every one of those extraordinary devices) and figuring out how you can place them to use for you.

In spite of the fact that Kali is unequivocally multi-reason, it is basically intended to help in entrance testing.

The goal of this book isn't to assist you with feeling comfortable when you use Kali Linux. In addition to helping improve your comprehension and streamlining your experience so when you are occupied with an infiltration test and time is of the essence, you won't have to stress over losing valuable minutes to put in new programming or empower another system administration. In this book, we will acquaint you first with Linux. After that, we will jump further as we acquaint you with the subtleties of Kali.

Linux so you know precisely what is happening in the engine.

This is important information to have, especially when you are attempting to work under tight time limitations. It isn't unusual to require this amount of information when you are getting set up, investigating an issue, battling to twist an apparatus to your will, parsing yield from a device, or utilizing Kali in a bigger scale condition.

Is This Book for You?

In the event that you are anxious to jump into the mentally rich and unbelievably interesting field of data security, and have legitimately chosen Kali Linux as an essential stage, this book will help you in that voyage. It is written to help first-time Linux clients, and Kali clients trying to develop their insight about the underpinnings of Kali. It is also for individuals who have utilized Kali for a considerable length of time yet who are hoping to formalize their learning, grow their utilization of Kali, and fill in holes in their insight.

Also, this book can fill in as a guide, specialized reference, and study help for those seeking the Kali Linux Certified Professional confirmation.

Terms

There are various basic terms that regularly come into use while examining infiltration testing. Various callings, specialized claims to fame, and even individuals from a similar group have somewhat various understandings of the terms utilized in this field. Hence, the accompanying terms and related definitions will be utilized in this book.

Entrance Testing, Pentesting

Entrance testing is the approach, procedure, and methodology utilized by analyzers inside explicit and affirmed rules to attempt to bypass a data frameworks insurance including vanquishing the coordinated security highlights of that framework. This sort of testing is related with evaluating the specialized, regulatory, and operational settings and controls of a framework.

Regular infiltration tests just evaluate the security of the data framework as it is manufactured. The objective system framework executives and staff might possibly realize that an infiltration test is occurring.

Red Team, Red Teaming

Red Teams reproduce a potential enemy in procedure and methods.

These groups are regularly bigger than an infiltration testing group and have a lot more extensive experience. Infiltration testing itself is frequently a sub-component of a Red Team Exercise, however, these activities test different elements of an association's security device. Red Teams frequently assault an association through specialized, social, and physical methods. They regularly utilize similar procedures utilized by Black Hat Hackers to test the association or data frameworks securities against these antagonistic on-screen characters. Notwithstanding Penetration Testing, the Red Team will perform Social Engineering assaults, including phishing and lance phishing and physical assaults including dumpster jumping and lock picking to pick up data and access. By and large, the objective associations staff won't realize a Red Team Exercise is being directed.

Moral Hacking

An Ethical Hacker is an expert infiltration analyzer that assaults frameworks in the interest of the framework proprietor or association owning the data framework. For the motivations behind this book, Ethical Hacking is synonymous with Penetration Testing.

White Hat

White Hat is a slang term for an Ethical Hacker or a PC security professional that believes in philosophies that improve the security of data frameworks.

Dark Hat

Dark Hat is a term that distinguishes an individual that utilizes specialized methods to sidestep a frameworks security without consent to carry out unethical actions. Entrance Testers and Red Team individuals regularly utilize the strategies utilized by Black Hats to mimic these people while directing approved activities or tests. Dark Hats direct their exercises without authorization and illicitly.

Dark Hat alludes to a specialized master that straddles the line between White Hat and Black Hat. These people regularly endeavor to sidestep the security highlights of a data framework without authorization, not for benefit but instead to make the framework overseers aware of found shortcomings. Dark Hats regularly don't have authorization to test frameworks, yet are generally not after money related additions.

Powerlessness Assessment, Vulnerability Analysis

A powerlessness examination is utilized to assess the security settings of a data framework. These kinds of appraisals incorporate the assessment of security patches applied to and missing from the framework. The Vulnerability Assessment Team, or VAT, can be outside of the data framework or part of the data framework's supporting staff.

Security Controls Assessment

Security Controls Assessments assess the data framework's consistency with explicit legitimate or administrative necessities. Instances of these prerequisites incorporate, yet are not restricted to, the Federal Information Security Management Act (FISMA), the Payment Card Industry (PCI), and Health Insurance Portability and Accountability Act (HIPAA). Security Control Assessments are utilized as a feature of the Body of Evidence (BOE) utilized by associations to approve a data framework for activity in a generation situation. A few frameworks require infiltration tests as a major aspect of the security control evaluation.

Noxious User Testing, Malicious User Testing

In Malicious User Testing, the assessors accept the job of believed insider acting malignantly, a vindictive client, or a maluser. In these tests, the assessor is given the certifications of an approved general or managerial client, typically as a test account. The assessor will utilize these qualifications to endeavor to sidestep security limitations remembering seeing archives and settings for a way the record was not approved, changing settings that ought not be changed, and raising their very own consents past the level the record ought to have. Malicious client testing recreates the activities of a maverick insider.

Social Engineering

Social Engineering assaults are typically hurtful to the data framework or client. The Social Engineer utilizes individuals' natural need to help other people to bargain their way into the data framework. Normal Social Engineering strategies include attempting to get help work area examiners to reset client account passwords or have end clients uncover their passwords empowering the Social Engineer to sign in to accounts they are not approved. Other Social Engineering strategies incorporate phishing and lance phishing.

Phishing

In Phishing (articulated like angling), the social architect endeavors to get the focused-on individual to uncover individual data like client names, account numbers, and passwords. This is frequently done by utilizing legitimate looking, but phony, messages from partnerships, banks, and client care staff. Different types of phishing attempt to get clients to tap on fake hyperlinks that will enable vindictive code to be introduced on the objective's PC without their knowledge. This malware will be utilized to extract information from the PC or utilize the PC to assault others. Phishing ordinarily isn't focused at explicit clients yet might be everybody on a mailing list or with a particular email address expansion, for instance each client with a "@foo.com" augmentation.

Lance Phishing

Lance Phishing is a type of phishing in which the objective clients are explicitly recognized. For instance, the aggressor may discover the email address of the Chief Executive Officer (CEO) of an organization or other officials and just phish these individuals.

Dumpster Diving

In Dumpster Diving, the assessor channels through refuse disposed of by framework clients searching for data that will prompt further comprehension of the objective. This data could be framework setups or settings, arrange charts, programming variants and equipment parts, and even client names and passwords. The term alludes to entering an enormous refuse holder, or "plunging" little office trash cans whenever the open door can produce rewarding data, too.

Live CD, Live Disk, or LiveOS

A live CD or live circle alludes to an optical plate that contains a whole working framework. These plates are helpful to numerous assessors and can be adjusted to contain explicit programming segments, settings, and instruments. While live circles are regularly found on Linux disseminations, a few Microsoft Windows forms have been discharged throughout the years. In view of the data framework's settings, live circles could be the main bit of hardware that the assessor or analyzer should bring to the appraisal as the objective framework's PCs can be booted to the live circle. This turns one of the data framework's resources against the framework itself.

KALI HISTORY

Kali Linux is the latest live circle security appropriation discharged by Offensive Security. This present rendition has more than 300 security and entrance testing devices included, sorted into supportive gatherings frequently utilized by entrance analyzers and others evaluating data frameworks. Not at all like prior disseminations discharged by Offensive Security, Kali Linux utilizes the Debian 7.0 conveyance as its base. Kali Linux proceeds with the genealogy of its antecedent, Backtrack, and is upheld by a similar group. As indicated by Offensive Security, the name change connotes the organization's complete revamp of the Backtrack dissemination. The tremendous enhancements over prior versions of the Backtrack appropriation justified an adjustment in name that shows this isn't only another rendition of Backtrack. Backtrack itself was an improvement over the two security devices it received from White Hat and SLAX (WHAX) also, Auditor. In this line, Kali Linux is the most recent manifestation of the business security examining and infiltration evaluation devices.

Downloading and Installing Kali Linux

Data IN THIS CHAPTER - This section will disclose how to get Kali Linux, one of the most dominant entrance testing tool boxes accessible.

Part OVERVIEW AND KEY LEARNING POINTS - This section will clarify the downloading and introducing process of Kali

Linux on:

Hard drives

Thumb drives (USB memory sticks)

SD cards

Kali Linux

Introducing working frameworks, for example, Microsoft's Windows, Apple's OS X, or open source stages like Debian and Ubuntu, might be natural to a few, however an update on this procedure is necessary. Those that have never introduced a working framework before ought not stress, the accompanying areas in this section will explain how to find, download, and introduce Kali Linux.

Kali Linux is remarkable from numerous points of view. However, the most significant qualifications of this conveyance are the capacity to run from a hard drive establishment as well as boot as a live plate and the number and kind of specific applications introduced as a matter of course. A live circle is a working framework introduced on a plate including Compact Disks (CDs), Digital Video Disk (DVD), or Blu-Ray Disk. As an entrance analyzer, the capacity to boot a live circle is very significant.

Those with access to neighborhood machines on the system can use live circles to utilize these machines regardless of whether the entrance analyzer doesn't have a record on the introduced working framework. The framework will boot to the live plate rather than the neighborhood hard drive; that is, on the off chance that the machine is arranged accurately the infiltration analyzer will, at that point, approach a large number of the assets on the nearby system, while simultaneously not leaving proof on the nearby machines hard drive. The product introduced on Kali Linux is extraordinarily equipped for the entrance analyzer. Of course, Kali Linux has 400 infiltration testing and security instruments, bundles and applications introduced and can include more as they are required.

Framework Information

Every working framework has slight deviations that will show up through their underlying establishment and arrangement; notwithstanding, most Linux/Unix-based stages are generally comparative in nature. When introducing Kali Linux, similarly as with other Linux working frameworks, arranging before establishment is pivotal. The following is a short rundown of interesting points when introducing Kali Linux.

- Will the working framework run on a PC or workstation?

- What size hard drive is required?

- Does the accessible hard drive have adequate space accessible?

- What number hard drive parcels are required?

- Is the executives log a worry?

- Is security a worry?

Choosing a Hardware Platform for Installation

Customarily, the working framework is introduced on the PC's hard drive. With working frameworks, for example, Kali Linux, there is a capacity to introduce the working framework to thumb drives (otherwise known as glimmer drives) and SD cards because of the ongoing accessibility, and reasonableness of bigger limit gadgets. Despite the capacity utilized to introduce the working framework, it is important to decide to introduce it to an independent PC, (for example, a lab PC) or a PC that will consider a versatile arrangement.

In the event that certain equipment, like powerful illustrations cards, will be utilized for splitting passwords, it is suggested that the establishment of Kali Linux be introduced on a personal computer. On the off chance that there is a need to convey the working framework from client site to client site, or there is a longing to test remote gadgets, a PC is prescribed. The establishment of the working framework is the equivalent for PC and personal computers.

Hard Drive Selection

Not to over utilize the expression, however "Size does make a difference." A general guideline is: the bigger the drive, the better. This book is suggesting a drive with at least 120 GB of room. Even this can turn out to be full rapidly, particularly on account of secret phrase splitting and crime scene investigation or pentesting ventures that require a great deal of command over, proof, logs and report age or assortment. On account of general business and government security evaluations, the working framework is cleaned, deleted, or totally evacuated to keep up a set in benchmark condition. This training is broadly acknowledged all through the security network because of the requirement for a legitimate treatment of client classified information and limiting spillage of corporate data that might hurt the organization's reputation.

Apportioning the Hard Drive

Apportioning is the demonstration of isolating out the document framework to explicit parts of the hard drive by setting extraordinary square sizes and divisions. Parceling can keep a working framework from getting undermined by log documents that assume control over a framework and in specific situations give more prominent security. The working framework is, at the fundamental level, effectively broken into two distinct segments.

The primary segment is the swap territory, which is utilized for memory paging and capacity. A subsequent segment is assigned for everything else and is designed with a record structure, for example, the all-inclusive document framework 3 (ext3) or expanded document framework 4 (ext4). On PCs, particularly those gadgets where the working framework will be reloaded on numerous occasions, further dividing isn't important. For altered establishments or PCs that will have an increasingly steady working framework, there is a need to, in any event, separate out the brief (tmp) documents.

Propelled dividing of the hard drive and double booting a PC are outside the extent of this book and won't be secured. The main exemption is in Appendix A where redone circulations are presented with a thirdparty application called, Tribal Chicken.

Security During Installation

Kali Linux is an exceptionally versatile working framework with plenty of pre-introduced apparatuses that can pulverize PCs or arrange foundation. Whenever utilized inappropriately or dishonestly, it can also prompt activities that will be seen as criminal or law breaking. Consequently, passwords are basic. While passwords are the most fundamental security practice, numerous chairmen and security experts frequently overlook or disregard the utilization of passwords. Fundamental security practices, for example, legitimate utilization of passwords, are basic to guarantee that your establishment of Kali Linux isn't used by other people who may coincidentally or malevolently cause damage to an individual, PC, or system.

Downloading Kali

Kali Linux is a conveyance of Linux and is downloaded in an ISO (pronounced: eye-so) record. It should be downloaded from another PC and afterward consumed to a circle before establishment. At the time of writing this book, Kali Linux can be downloaded from http://www.kali.org/downloads/.

Documentation for cutting edge tasks, designs, and unique cases can likewise be found in Kali's legitimate site, http://www.kali.org/official-documentation/. There is likewise an exceptionally huge and dynamic network where clients can post questions and help other people with challenges. Enlistment at this site is prescribed to access the network sheets that are overseen by Hostile Security, the creators of Kali Linux. Hostile Security will likewise convey messages about updates and network data.

Make certain to choose the correct design (i386 5 32-piece, amd64 5 64-piece). The trusted contributed pictures of Kali Linux are outside the scope of this book. If you wish to get acquainted with Kali, or need a sandbox domain for more noteworthy control, then the VMware download is ideal for those circumstances. Snap on the suitable download connection to proceed with your choice.

For Microsoft Windows 7 clients, double tap on the finished download and the Burn ISO Wizard will show up. Pursue the prompts to finish the transformation of ISO picture to a DVD that can be utilized for establishment. Linux clients should open the ISO in an appropriate plate consuming application, for example, K3b.

Hard Drive Installation

The accompanying sections will give a literary and graphical establishment manage intended for straightforwardness. To effectively introduce Kali on the framework's hard drive, or even boot to the live circle, it is important that the Basic Input Output System (BIOS) be set to boot from optical plate. To start the establishment, place the CD in the PC's CD plate and boot the PC to the circle. Propelled clients alright with virtualization innovation, for example, VMware's Player or Oracle's Virtual box will likewise discover this guide direct and supportive to making a virtualized variant of Kali Linux.

Booting Kali with a PC booted to the Kali Linux circle effectively will show a screen that seems to be like a Figure. The rendition of Kali Linux being utilized for this guide is 1.0.5 64-Bit; variants downloaded at various occasions may look marginally changed; be that as it may, the graphical establishments are very comparable in nature. A refreshed guide for each new arrival of Kali Linux can be found at http://www.kali.org/ and it is strongly suggested to visit this site for the most recent documentation for your form before establishment or in case of questions.

Kali Linux is disseminated as a "Live CD" (otherwise known as Live ISO), which implies that the working framework can be run directly from the plate notwithstanding being introduced to a hard drive. Running Kali from the live circle enables the framework for sure and the entirety of the apparatuses will execute; be that as it may, the working framework displayed is non-determined. Non steady implies that once the PC is closed down, any memory, spared settings, archives, and potentially significant work or research might be lost. Running Kali in a non-determined state takes extraordinary consideration, propelled dealing with, and nice comprehension of the Linux directions and working framework. This technique is best for learning the Linux working framework without erasing the current working framework previously introduced on the PC's hard drive.

Another establishment that is out of the scope of this book, is Installation with Speech Synthesis. This is a fresher component to Kali and the Debian working framework. Establishment can be controlled vocally if you have equipment that supports discourse amalgamation. This book will concentrate on the graphical establishment for the present; in this manner, feature Graphical Install and press the Enter key.

Establishment—Setting the Defaults

The following screens will permit the choice of the framework's default language, area, and console language. Select the suitable settings and keep on propelling the installer. As the PC starts to pre-organize the establishment of Kali Linux, different advancement bars will come on the screen all through the establishment. Choosing the default settings is proper for the vast majority of those screens.

Establishment—Initial Network Setup

Figured subtleties the underlying arrangement and fundamental setup of the essential system interface card. Pick a host name by composing in the container and tapping on Continue. Host names ought to be one of a kind, as entanglements with systems administration can be a consequence of PCs that were designed with a similar host name while on a similar system.

After choosing a host name and hitting the Continue button, the following screen will request the PC's completely qualified space name, FQDN. This is essential for joining space conditions and a bit much for most lab situations. For this guide, the FQDN was left deliberately clear and can be skirted by choosing the Continue button.

Passwords

The following brief in the wizard will request a root-level secret phrase. The default secret word is: toor; in any case, another secret key must be chosen that contains every one of the following: capitalized, lowercase, number, and image. The secret word ought to have no detectability to the client and not be effectively speculated. A secret word of at least 10 characters is recommended. For instance, if the client once played secondary school soccer, a password like soccer22 would not be prescribed. Passwords can be produced using varieties of basic expressions to build review. Here are a few instances of solid passwords:

- St0n(3)b@tt73 "Stone Battle"

- P@p3r0kCur5# "Paper, Rock, Curse"
- m!gh7yP@jjjama% h "Forceful Pajamas"

When composing your secret phrase, it will appear as a progression of bullets.

This is typical and conceals your secret phrase from being shown on the PC screen. After entering the equivalent solid secret word twice, click on Continue to progress further into the program.

Arranging the System Clock shows the brief for choosing a time period zone. Click on the suitable time zone and the Continue button.

Apportioning Disks

There are such a significant number of approaches to arrange segments for setting up a Linux working framework that a whole book could be written on the subject. This guide will concentrate on the most essential establishment, Guided Partitioning.

A few pictures show the default settings to that are at first featured. There will be nothing to choose until a specific Figure. Right now, the establishment might be accelerated by clicking Proceed until apportioning is finished. It is shrewd to survey each progression of the establishment wizard.

A few pictures show various choices for dividing hard drives during the establishment. LVM, or Logical Volume Management, isn't suggested for workstation, thumb drive, or SD card establishment. LVM is for various hard drives, and is prescribed distinctly for cutting edge clients. "Guided—client whole circle," ought to be chosen. Click on Continue to progress through the establishment procedure. A figure shows the hard drive that has been chosen for establishment.

Contingent upon your equipment and form of Kali Linux, the establishment experience may contrast somewhat. The hard drive will be chosen for; if needed, click on the Continue button to progress through the establishment procedure. As this book is designed for new clients of the Kali Linux dispersion: "All records in a single parcel (suggested for new clients)" is the best alternative and ought to be chosen. Click on the Continue button to progress through the establishment procedure.

At this point in the wizard, the parcel direct has been finished and is introduced for your survey. An essential parcel containing the entirety of the framework, client, and scripting documents will be made as one segment. A subsequent segment is made for swap space. The swap zone is virtual framework memory that pages records to and from the PC's focal preparing unit (CPU) and arbitrary access memory (RAM). All Linux frameworks are prescribed to have a swap zone and the general practice is to set the swap zone equivalent to or one and a half times the measure of physical RAM introduced on the PC. As found in the figure, "Get done with parceling and compose changes to circle," will be chosen for you. Click on Continue to progress through the establishment procedure. Some figure is a last possibility audit for parceling before the hard drive arrangement is submitted. There are approaches to change segment estimates later on if needed, yet doing so might cause enormous harm to your working framework if not done accurately. This brief in the wizard is an admonition that you are going to compose information to a predefined hard drive with the recently characterized parcel tables. Select YES and click on Continue to progress through the establishment procedure.

After clicking Continue at the last brief of the parceling area of the wizard, the hard drive segment will start. An A figure shows that the genuine establishment is being led as of now. Depending upon the equipment you have, this procedure can take only a few moments to an hour or more.

Arrange the Package Manager

The bundle supervisor is an essential piece of the working framework's arrangement. The bundle supervisor alludes to the update vault where Kali Linux will pull updates and security patches. It is prescribed to utilize the system reflect that accompanies the Kali Linux ISO as this will the most state-of-the-art hotspots for bundle the executives. The figure shows that "YES" will be chosen. Click on the Continue button to progress through the establishment procedure.

In the case of utilizing an intermediary, enter the arrangement data where fitting on the following brief in the wizard or leave it blank. Click on Continue.

Introducing the GRUB Loader

The Grand Unified Bootloader (GRUB) is the primary screen that will be shown each time the PC is begun. This permits the check of specific settings at boot, make on the fly changes, and make setting modifications before the working framework loads. While GRUB isn't fundamental for some propelled clients, it is strongly suggested for most establishment types. Click on "YES" to introduce the GRUB, then click on Continue.

Finishing the Installation

Presently remove the plate from the PC and reboot. When prompted, do as such and afterward click on the Continue catch to complete the establishment.

After rebooting, the Welcome screen will be exhibited. Sign in as the root client with the predefined password set earlier in the establishment procedure. Welcome to Kali Linux!

Thumb Drive Installation

USB memory gadgets, regularly alluded to as thumb drives, are simply a capacity gadget that is joined through a USB interface to the PC. This book suggests utilizing a USB gadget with at least 8GB of space, ideally considerably more. New PCs can boot to USB gadgets. If this alternative is chosen, ensure that the PC being utilized can bolster booting from a USB gadget.

The accompanying areas separate the establishment of Kali Linux on to USB utilizing a Microsoft Windows PC or Linux stage. Make certain to check the documentation given on the Official Kali Linux landing page for updates to this procedure.

With regards to thumb drives being utilized as bootable gadgets, there are two key terms that are significant: determination and non-persistence. Constancy alludes to the capacity of your gadget to hold any composed or adjusted records after the machine is turned off. Non - persistence alludes to the gadget losing all settings, customizations, and records if the machine reboots or is turned off. Explicitly for this book, the thumb drive establishment of Kali Linux from a Windows stage will be non-persistent, and the establishment from a Linux stage will be constant.

Windows (Nonpersistent)

Required application—Win32 Disk Imager: http://sourceforge.net/ventures/win32diskimager/

Before downloading the Kali Linux ISO, put a thumb drive in the PC and wait for it to be identified by Windows, observing the drive letter relegated. Next open Win32 Disk Imager. Click on the envelope symbol to peruse and choose the Kali ISO document and afterward click the "alright" button. Select the right drive letter from the gadget drop-down menu. At long last click the "State" button.

When Win32 Disk Imager has finished consuming the ISO, reboot the PC and select the thumb drive from the BIOS POST menu. Most makers have various strategies for booting to USB gadgets; make certain to check the PC producer's documentation.

Linux (Persistent)

When constructing a steady thumb drive, again, size does make a difference! The greater the thumb drive capacity, the better. Additionally, contingent upon the rendition of Linux in which you will assemble this USB gadget, be certain that the application GParted is introduced. Check your working framework's documentation if you are experiencing issues introducing GParted. One of the accompanying techniques might be fundamental for your Linux establishment if GParted isn't introduced:

- well-suited get introduce gparted

- fitness introduces gparted

- yum introduce gparted

Subsequent to downloading the Kali Linux ISO, plug in your thumb drive. Open a terminal window and confirm the USB gadgets area the accompanying direction. mount j grep - l udisks jawk '{print $1}'

Shows that the yield of the order as "/dev/sdb1." The USB gadget's yield might be diverse dependent on the PCs settings and design. In the following order, swap "sdb" to coordinate the right distinguishing proof and evacuate any numbers toward the end. Utilize the "dd" order to move the Kali ISO picture to the USB gadget. dd if 5 kali_linux_image.iso of 5/dev/sdb bs 5 512k Now dispatch Gparted. gparted/dev/sdb. The drive should as of now have one parcel with the picture of Kali that was simply introduced.

Add another parcel to the USB by choosing New, from the menu that shows up in the wake of clicking on the Partition menu from the File

Menu Bar. Slight deviations in yield can be available from various gadget producers. By and large, the means are like the following:

- Click on the dim "unallocated" space.

- Click on "New" from the Partition drop-down menu.

- Use the sliders or physically determine drive size.

- Set the File System to ext4.

- Click Add.

- From the primary window select, Apply All Operations from the Edit dropdown menu.

- Click Okay when prompted. This may take some time.

To include constant usefulness utilize the accompanying order. mkdir/mnt/usb mount/dev/sdb2/mnt/usb reverberation "/association".. /mnt/usb/persistence.confumount/mnt/usb

34

Formation of the LiveUSB is currently finished. Reboot the PC and boot from the thumb drive.

SD Card Installation

Micro computing gadgets, for example, the RaspberryPi and Google's Chrome Notebook, are fit for running on SD cards. These little gadgets can be utilized for plenty of purposes; a person is just restricted by their very own creative mind. The best of the gadgets, for example, the Raspberry Pi, is that they are modest and an enormous hit in the open source networks making assets promptly accessible to tinkerers all over the place.

There is one disadvantage to the introducing Kali Linux on ARM gadgets; the pictures are custom and must be characterized for each bit of equipment.

Pictures for ARM gadgets can be situated on Kali's legitimate download pages, http://www.kali.org/downloads/. Check whether your equipment has an upheld picture accessible for download.

The following gives a short manual for introducing Kali Linux to good ARM engineering-based gadgets.

1. Download the suitable picture from Kali's legitimate site (http://www.kali.org/downloads/).

2. Add a blank SD card. Confirm the mounted area with the accompanying direction. mount j grep - I vfat (Assuming/dev/sdb for the following stage.)

3. Move the Kali.img document to the SD card. dd if 5 kali.img of 5/dev/sdb bs 5 512k

4. Unmount and match up any compose tasks before extracting the gadget. umount/dev/sdb adjust

5. Extract the SD card.

6. Supplement the SD card containing the Kali Linux picture into your ARM engineering registering gadget and boot to the SD card.

In this section, the themes secured will enable the client to introduce Kali Linux to most PCs, workstations, thumb drives, and smaller scale figuring gadgets. Introducing Kali Linux is a lot of like riding a bike; do it once, and you won't generally ever forget how to introduce Kali in the future. Check with the documentation and network message sheets on Kali's authentic site for new updates, variants, and advancements created in the security network. Connecting up and coordinating with other security experts, specialists, and programmers can, and will, grow the psyche, help you dive further into new tasks, and aid answer addresses when capable.

Programming, Patches, and Upgrades

Data IN THIS CHAPTER

- APT Package Handling Utility

- Debian Package Manager

- Tar-balls

- A Practical Guide to Installing Nessus

Section OVERVIEW AND KEY LEARNING POINTS - This part will explore the procedure important for looking after, updating, and introducing custom and outsider applications utilizing APT bundle dealing with utility (adept get) and the Debian bundle supervisor (dpkg).

Well-Suited Package Handling Utility

The APT bundle dealing with utility, known as "able get," is a lightweight and amazingly incredible order line device for introducing and evacuating programming bundles. Able get monitors everything introduced alongside the required conditions, which are the extra programming bundles required for appropriate usefulness of other programming. For example, Metasploit, the pentester's closest companion, depends on a specific programming language called Ruby. Without Ruby introduced, Metasploit couldn't dispatch; subsequently, Ruby is a reliance of Metasploit.

Able get does not just monitor the conditions for introduced programming. It will monitor forming and entomb conditions when updates are accessible. At the point when programming bundles are never again valuable or deteriorated well-suited get will caution the client at the next refresh and prompt to expel old bundles.

Able get can be an extremely basic or exceptionally involved apparatus. The organization of bundles is pivotal to ensuring Kali Linux works appropriately and that product bundles are state-of-the-art. While the average client of Kali Linux doesn't have to know the inside operations of well-suited get, there are a few rudiments that each client should know.

Introducing Applications or Packages

Introducing extra programming is the most essential capacity of the able get order and is straightforward. The linguistic structure below will give an example of the fundamental use of the introduce subcommand:

adept get introduce {package_name}

Take a stab at introducing "gimp;" a picture altering programming bundle: well-suited get introduce gimp

Update

Now and again the sources, or vaults, should be checked for updates to different applications and bundles introduced on Kali Linux. Updates should be checked before introducing any new bundles, and is needed before playing out a move up to the working framework or programming applications or bundles. The punctuation for performing refreshes pursues: adept get update

Redesign

No framework is ever great. Each major working framework is in a consistent condition of progress, improvement, and fixing the executives to offer new highlights or fix bugs. The update capacity will pull down and introduce all new bundled variants of new introduced programming bundles. The magnificence of all Linux based working frameworks is that they're open source, implying that anybody on the planet can submit new code to the dispersion directors of the working framework to help improve the usefulness of the framework for bug detection or a requirement for development. This takes into account patches to be refreshed quicker contrasted with the corporate monsters like Microsoft. As expressed before, it is necessary to install an update before running an overhaul. To update Kali utilize the accompanying direction:

adept get update

Appropriation Upgrade

The appropriation update work works comparably to the overhaul work. This capacity likewise searches out hotspots for extraordinary stamped bundles and their conditions just as new bundles the dissemination directors have assigned to be incorporated with the most current gauge. For instance, while conjuring the circulation overhaul work, the whole form of Kali will be raised from variant 1.0 to rendition 1.n, or 2.n, etc. Use the accompanying language to update Kali: well-suited get dist-update

Expel

Able get can be utilized to diminish the impression of a framework, or when evacuating free of a particular program. It is additionally recommended that all bundles not being used, those not filling a need, or redundant for your working framework, be uninstalled. For instance, if the Leaf cushion application isn't required on the framework, at that point expel it. If the application should be introduced later, it tends to be, notwithstanding, it is ideal to forget about what is pointless. The accompanying language can be utilized to expel an application or bundle: able get expel {package_name}

Have a go at expelling "leafpad" and afterward reinstalling the application:

able get expel leafpad

able get introduce leafpad

Auto Remove

After some time, the working framework's application bundles are supplanted with better than ever forms. The auto expel capacity will expel old bundles that are never again required for the best possible usefulness of the framework. It is prescribed that the auto expel work be pursued before an overhaul or appropriation update. Utilize the accompanying language to run auto evacuate:

able get autoremove

Cleanse

What is the distinction between expel and cleanse? The expel capacity won't demolish any design documents, and leaves those things on your hard drive in the event that the records are required later. This is valuable, particularly with applications, for example, MySQL, Samba

Server, or Apache. The setup records are critical for the operability of your applications. Sometimes, it is important to expel the entirety of the application documents, even design records for that application, from the framework so as to re-introduce applications to a clear state and begin once again, or clear all hints of potentially delicate data. Cleansing an application from the framework will totally eradicate the application bundle and all related setup records in a single motion. Be careful to not get too careless when utilizing the cleanse work; it is hazardous when utilized inaccurately or on an inappropriate application as all related records will be expelled from the framework. Cleanse can be utilized with the accompanying language structure: well-suited get cleanse {package_name}

Clean

Bundles are downloaded to the framework from their source, unpackaged, and afterward introduced. The bundles will live on the framework until further notice.

These bundles are never again fundamental after establishment of the application. After some time, these bundles can gobble up plate space and should be cleaned away. The accompanying linguistic structure can be utilized to start the perfect capacity: able get spotless

Autoclean

Autocleaning additionally cleans the framework along these lines as the perfect capacity. It ought to be used for overhaul and conveyance moves up to the framework, as the autoclean capacity will evacuate old bundles that have been supplanted with new ones. For example, assume application Y form 1 was introduced on the framework and after a move up to the framework, application Y v1 is supplanted with application Y v2. The autoclean capacity will just clean away form 1, while, the perfect capacity will expel the application bundles for the two variants. The following language structure will begin the autoclean work: adept get autoclean

Assembling It All

Organization of bundles is tied in with working more efficiently. The following are the accompanying directions that a client can use to ensure that the entirety of the potential fixes, bundles, and updates are forward-thinking and all set:

1. well-suited get update && adept get redesign && well-suited get dist -overhaul

2. well-suited get autoremove && adept get autoclean

The "&&" passage on the order line considers numerous directions to run successively.

Debian Package Manager

The significant flavors (or disseminations) of Linux have singular application bundling frameworks. Kali Linux was based over the Debian 7.0 base working framework, and may require outsider applications, like Tenable's Nessus.

Nessus is a weakness-examining application that can be introduced from prepackaged documents appropriate for the Debian Package Manager. The utilization of Nessus will be explored in the section on examining. While downloading these sorts of uses, search for the ".deb" document expansion toward the finish of the record name.

There is no advantage of utilizing the Debian Package Manager over APT. The aptget program was composed explicitly for the administration of Debian bundles.

Outside applications that must be purchased from a seller are not accessible freely and well-suited gets sources will be not able find the bundles for download and establishment. Kali Linux isn't equipped for handling RPM (Red Hat Packages) without additional product introduced, and the act of utilizing RPMs on a Debian-based framework isn't suggested.

Introduce

In the wake of downloading a .deb bundle, the dpkg direction should be utilized so as to introduce the bundle. Most .deb bundles are clear and contain the entirety of the conditions needed for the application to work effectively. In some cases, for the most part managing authorized programming, merchants may require extra strides before establishment and will by and large have guidelines for appropriate establishment on the framework. Make certain to check the seller's documentation before beginning the establishment:

dpkg - I {package_name.deb}/{target_directory}

Expel

Expelling a bundle (- r) or cleansing a bundle (- P) works in the generally same way that APT does and pursues a similar example for dealing with bundles: dpkg - r {package_name.deb}

Cleansing a bundle with the Debian bundle chief works similarly to the evacuate work and can be started with the accompanying direction:

dpkg - p {package_name.deb}

Checking for Installed Package

One super power that APT doesn't have over the Debian Package Manager is the capacity to decipher the present status of introduced or evacuated programming. When utilizing the rundown work inside dpkg, the yield will show a few characters code toward the start of the line demonstrating the bundle's present condition of establishment. When run against the Leaf cushion application bundle, the accompanying picture shows that the bundle is evacuated, yet the arrangement documents are as yet accessible.

After the order dpkg - P leafpad is run, the bundle's design documents are likewise expelled. Figure 3.2 shows the comparing yield of the Leafpad application bundle when it has been totally cleansed from the framework. To search for the status of introduced or expelled programming, utilize this language structure: dpkg - l {package_name}

Progressively point by point data about the bundle introduced can be shown on the screen with the following order:

Give close consideration to the utilization of upper and lowercase. Lowercase "p" prints the data to the screen. The capitalized "P" will cleanse the bundle from the framework without asking, "Are you certain?"

Tarballs

Tar, starting in the yester long periods of Unix frameworks, was named for its capacity, which was at first for composing numerous documents to Tape Archives (TAR).

Not every person needs the capacity to move various records to tape. However, they might need the characteristic usefulness of the tar application which is to produce a holder document that will house different documents. This allows simpler shipping of documents. Moreover, these documents can be compacted with gunzip (gzip) diminishing their general size. A few bundles from outsider or opensource activities can be downloaded in tarball design and are effectively distinguished by the .tar record augmentation or .tar.gz for compacted tarballs.

During an infiltration test, a gigantic measure of filtering archives, screen catches, redid contents, and customer documentation are caught. Utilizing the Tarball framework takes into consideration simpler assortment, the board, and payment, everything being equal. It is additionally exceptionally recommended that all records from entrance tests be kept in a protected area for 5 years, or the date dictated by the legal time limit of the state where the work was performed. Clients may likewise have stipulations on maintenance prerequisites that ought to be explained in the infiltration tests rules of commitment (ROE). The ROE will be explored in the section on announcing. If an organization or contractual worker is exceptionally dynamic with infiltration testing, the measure of documentation can heap up rapidly and before long be wild. Tarball, particularly when compacted, gives an arrangement of control that keeps records separated and takes into consideration simpler reinforcement and administration.

Formation of a Tarball

Making a tarball record can be clear or complex. Keep in mind, the first capacity of the tar direction was intended to send records to TAR. For cutting edge use of the tarball framework, look at the manual pages for tarball (man tarball). For this book just the fundamental formation of tarball records will be incorporated; be that as it may, this data is helpful and can progress to pretty much any Linux-based stage. The following gives a look through the steps needed that a client can pursue to make an example tarball.

Make an index for your documents. For this situation the tar-demo1 catalog is being made with the mkdir order: mkdir tar-demo1

Next make various records in this index that can be utilized to delineate the tar direction. For this situation the correct carrot (.) will be utilized to make a record with the substance "Hi world." This document will be named record 1, and a number of records can be made in a similar way by changing the last number. Making the records along these lines will likewise move your documents into the registry indicated, for this situation tar-demo1: reverberation "Hi World". tar-demo1/file1

49

reverberation "Hi World". tar-demo1/record 2

Change into the registry that you wish to make a tarball in. For this example it is the tar-demo1 index:

album tar-demo1

Produce another tarball with the documents contained inside the present catalog.

In this model the reference bullet (*) is utilized to mean everything in this registry ought to be added to the tar document:

tar - cf tarball-demo.tar *

The tar - tf order is utilized to list the substance of the tarball:

tar - tf tarball-demo.tar

Extricating Files from a Tarball

The steps to removing records from a tarball are as simple as one, two, and three; be that as it may, the area of the data is put that is the key.

The documents extricated from a tarball are set in the working registry. If a tarball is removed from the root index, that is the place the documents are going to wind up. It is prescribed that great propensities structure at the earliest opportunity; in this manner, all clients of tarballs should utilize the "- C" switch when extricating records. The "- C" switch enables the client to determine the area of where the documents need to go.

Make an index for the records to be extricated into. For this situation the registry made is named tar-demo2:

mkdir/root/tar-demo2

Concentrate the records into the particular catalog:

tar - xf/root/tar-demo1/tarball-demo.tar - C/root/tar-demo2/

Ensure that all of the records are removed to the registry that was indicated in the prior advance:

ls/root/tarball-demo2/

Packing a Tarball

Tarballs can be packed during creation with numerous various sorts of calculations. One standard being used is gunzip, otherwise called gzip.

This is finished with the accompanying directions.

Make a catalog for your documents. For this situation the tar-demo3 registry is made:

mkdir tar-demo3

Presently move your records into the index. As above the reverberation direction will be utilized to make the documents for this showing:

reverberation "Hi World". tar-demo3/file1

Change into the catalog that you wish to place your tarball. Again, in this model the tar-demo3 catalog is being utilized:

compact disc tar-demo3

Create another tarball with the documents contained inside the present index.

This is finished using the - czf switches with the tar order. The switches on the tar direction guarantee the tarball is made accurately. The c switch makes another chronicle and the z guarantees the records are packed (or compressed) and the f switch means the name following the switches (tarball-demo.tar.gz) will be utilized as the name for the new document. Again, the reference mark (*) tells tar that everything in this index ought to be remembered for the new tar record:

tar - czf tarball-demo.tar.gz *

Posting the substance of the tarball is finished with the t and f switches. The t switch shows the record substance ought to be shown (or composed to the screen) and again the f switch demonstrates the document name will pursue the switches:

tar - tf tarball-demo.tar

Extraction of documents from a packed tarball works the very same route as extraction from a non-compacted tarball. The main change is the x switch is utilized to show that tar should remove the substance of the tarball. While it isn't required, it is standard practice to name the record with the .gz augmentation to show to others that the tarball is packed. Notice that the record in this model has two periods (.tar.gz); this is absolutely adequate in Linux situations and is standard with packed tar documents:
tar - xf {tarball_file.tar.gz} - C {directory_for_files}

A Practical Guide To Installing Nessus

Viable, a well regarded name in the security network, has delivered a stunning application for defenselessness filtering called Nessus. There are two versions of the application that offer contrasting degrees of usefulness and backing. These are the Nessus Professional and Home forms. The Professional form offers significantly more modules for compliancy checking, SCADA, and arrangement checking and is amazing for group use. For this book, the establishment of the Nessus Vulnerability Scanner with the home feed will be utilized. Nessus is examined further in the part on filtering yet introducing Nessus now will concrete the information from this section.

Refresh and Clean the System Prior to Installing Nessus.

In a windows terminal type the following directions: well-suited get update && well-suited get redesign && able get dist-overhaul able get autoremove && well-suited get autoclean

Introduce and Configure Nessus

Download Nessus 5.0 or higher from http://www.nessus.org/download.

Select the Debian bundle for either 32-or 64-piece working framework. Peruse the membership understanding and click the Agree button.

Nessus will not work if the understanding isn't acknowledged. Note the area where the document is being downloaded to as it will be needed to finish the establishment.

From a terminal window enter the accompanying:

dpkg - I B/{Download_Location}/Nessus-{version}.deb

A progressively far reaching arrangement guide can be found in Appendix some time setting up a pentesting domain structure with Tribal Chicken.

End

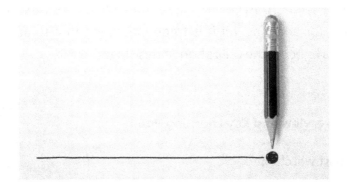

This section secured the basic abilities important for bundle the executives on the Kali Linux framework. Able is a ground-breaking order line apparatus that robotizes the administration of bundles, update, and fixes. The Debian Package Manager (dpkg) is the fundamental framework that APT was based over for bundling the executives. With the fundamental understanding and general acclimation of these instruments, anybody can stay up with the latest applications.

For cutting edge utilization of the instruments in this section, consult the manual pages either from inside a terminal window or online through their individual authority sites. These instruments can produce a domain ideal for any individual or pulverize a whole framework without a solitary brief or thought of regret. It is a very good idea that until a client is OK with the utilization of these apparatuses, that hands-on training ought to be practiced in a different framework or a virtual domain.

Designing Kali Linux

Data IN THIS CHAPTER - Using the default Kali Linux settings can be helpful for adapting yet it is frequently important to adjust essential settings to boost the utilization of this stage

Part Overview and Key Learning Points

This part will clarify

- the nuts and bolts of systems administration

- utilizing the graphical UI to arrange organize interfaces

- utilizing the direction line to design arrange interfaces

- utilizing the graphical UI to design remote cards

- utilizing the order line to design remote cards

- beginning, halting, and restarting the Apache server

- introducing an FTP server

- beginning, halting, and restarting the SSH server

- mounting outside media

- refreshing Kali

- redesigning Kali

- including the Debian store

ABOUT THIS CHAPTER - Networking is the way that PCs and other current electronic gadgets speak with one another. This can be viewed as streets between gadgets with rules and necessities (conventions), transit regulations (rule sets and arrangements), support groups (organize administrations), law enforcement (organize security), private streets (firewall ports and convention limitations—likewise part of security). In the following areas, the rudiments of systems administration will be portrayed as will the means that should be taken to appropriately design organizing in Kali.

Systems administration is a perplexing point, and this part scarcely starts to expose organizing. The clarification introduced here just serves to outline and disclose the segments required to effectively arrange the system parts of Kali Linux. To get an increasingly nitty gritty comprehension of systems administration look at *Networking Explained*, second ed., by Michael Gallo and William Hancock. This clarification will furnish the user with the fundamental comprehension of the most essential system segments.

The Basics of Networking

Systems administration can be thought of as a progression of electronic streets between PCs. These streets can be physical, most normally copper class 5 or 6 (CAT 5 or CAT 6) links or fiber optic links. Remote systems administration utilizes unique radio transmitters and collectors to direct indistinguishable fundamental errands from physical systems.

Notwithstanding the medium, physical or remote systems administration has similar fundamental parts. First there are at least two gadgets that will communicate, for instance, Adam's PC will speak with Bill's PC. To do this, they will require the right interchanges gear working on the right medium. For this model, Adam will interface the equivalent physical CAT5-based system that Bill is associated with. If the settings are right, Bill could be utilizing a remote system card and Adam could be utilizing a wired system card as long as the conventions and settings for both are right. For this to work accurately both Adam and Bill should interface a similar system portion utilizing a gadget like a remote switch that would associate the diverse physical media types, wired and remote.

There are various parts that make up a cutting edge organize and completely clarifying systems administration is a long way past the scope of this book. The little system portion that will be disclosed will be adequate to depict how to arrange a system card. This little system is just two PCs that are being utilized by Adam and Bill, a wired switch associated with a link modem and the links that interface everything together (all CAT5 in this model). The switch has an inside Internet convention (IP) address of 192.168.1.1, which is very normal for little home office (SOHO) and home systems default setup. This little switch interfaces with the Internet through its outside association, utilizing an IP address allocated by the Internet Service Provider that will empower Adam and Bill to surf the web once they effectively arrange their system cards. In this model, the switch likewise gives dynamic host design convention (DHCP), essential firewall capacities, and space name administration (DNS), every one of these will be talked about in more detail later. This system is shown in Figure 4.3 and will be the base system utilized in the entirety of the accompanying parts.

Private Addressing

The interior interface (or system card) for the switch has an IP address of 192.168.1.1; this is what is known as a private location as it can't be utilized on the Internet. It is fine for the interior system spoke to by the dark box in a Figure similar to the addresses given by DHCP, like the IP address given to Adam and Bill's PCs. A table records the normal private IP that can be utilized for interior or private systems, however can't be utilized on the Internet.

To get to the Internet, the switch does a touch of enchantment called arrange address interpretation (NAT) that changes over the IP used by Adam and Bill to addresses that can be used on the Internet. This is ordinarily the location that is given to the switch by the digital Internet supplier and will be relegated to the outer interface (another system card). If a client was to attempt to utilize these addresses on the Internet, without a NAT switch, the correspondence would bomb as Internet switches and different gadgets dismiss these private IP addresses.

Default Gateway

The switch isolates these two systems, inside and outer, and gives some fundamental security capacities, similar to a simple firewall. Moreover, the switch gives an exit from the private system to general society arrange, regularly the Internet. Thus, the switch's interior interface IP address is the exit from Adam and Bill's system. This location, called the default passage, will be utilized later when designing the system cards for the client's two PCs. A decent method to picture the default door is to see it as the single street out of a community. Anybody needing to leave the town would need to know where this street is. On a system PCs (through the system card) need to know where the exit from the neighborhood organize is; this is the default entryway.

Name Server

PCs converse with one another in numbers, while individuals are vastly improved at speaking with words and expressions. For correspondence to work effectively, PCs regularly utilize name server or area name administration (DNS). This book will cover DNS in more prominent detail later, so just an outline of DNS will be talked about in this section. Fundamentally, the name server interprets human cordial names (like www.syngress.com) to an IP address that PCs and systems administration segments are better at working with. The DNS, synonymous with name server, gives interpretation between human benevolent and PC well-disposed locations. For instance, when a PC needs to speak with another PC, a web server for instance, it should initially interpret the intelligible location to a PC neighborly address that can be utilized to send the message. The individual would type www.syngress.com in their preferred program, and the PC would advance this location for goals to a DNS machine. The DNS would answer with the machine facilitating the website page's IP address (69.163.177.2). The client's PC would then utilize this IP address to speak with the Syngress web server and the client could cooperate with the Syngress website page. Without this administration, people would be required to remember each site's special IP Address. This would mean individuals would need to recall 69.163.177.2, not syngress.com. Manual design of a system card requires the distinguishing proof of a DNS or name server.

DHCP

For unadulterated system enchantment, nothing beats DHCP. With a PC set up for programmed setup of DHCP, the client should simply interface with a working system link and get down to business. This is done when the PC starts correspondence over the system, by conveying a communicate demand searching for a DHCP server. The server reacts to the customer and allocates organizing designs to the mentioning PC. This incorporates an IP address for the PC (just the system card, yet that is a little in the weeds for this clarification), the default entryway, name server—or name servers, and the default subnet cover.

As a rule, this is an incredible method to arrange your system card. If you are leading an entrance test, utilizing DHCP to design your system card reports to everybody that you are entering the system, ordinarily not something to be thankful for.

Essential Subnetting

Subnetting is a subject that can confound many individuals, so for this book subnetting might be disclosed as the best approach to design organizes in the most ideal manner to spare IP addresses. This is finished by applying a cover that will sift through a portion of the PC's IP address permitting the systems tending to be revealed. Back to the Syngress model, the IP address is 69.163.177.2 and if we were on a little system that had under 255 clients we could utilize a class C subnet cover of 255.255.255.0. While applying the cover, portions of the location are counteracted and others remain, enabling the PCs on the system to know the system they are on. Again, a fundamental case of a subnet veil utilizes just the numbers 255 and 0 numbering octets; consequently, to distinguish the system, any piece of the location coordinated with a 255 isn't changed in any way, so the initial three octets of the IP address (69, 163, 177) will all be coordinated with 255 enabling the first numbers to be gone through. Any number coordinated with 0 is completely counteracted, so the last octet of the location, or 2, would be offset bringing about a 0. So by applying the subnet cover of 255.255.255.0 to the location 69.163.177.2, we find that the system address is 69.163.177.0. In most little systems, a subnet cover of 255.255.255.0 will function admirably, while bigger systems will require an alternate subnet veil that may have been determined to give administrations to a particular number of system has.

Kali Linux Default Settings

As clarified before, most entrance test engineers and white hat programmers, won't need their system card to report their essence on the system when the PC associates. This is exactly what Kali Linux will do when it is controlled up and interfaces with a system. Care must be taken when directing an infiltration test to dodge this unneeded additional correspondence by crippling the system card before connecting to the system. With custom introduces including to a hard drive, thumb drive, or SD card, this programmed system design can be changed. Another approach to change this is by building a custom live plate that will be arranged for manual system setup. These techniques will all be examined in Chapter 5 on tweaking Kali Linux.

Utilizing the Graphical User Interface to Configure Network Interfaces

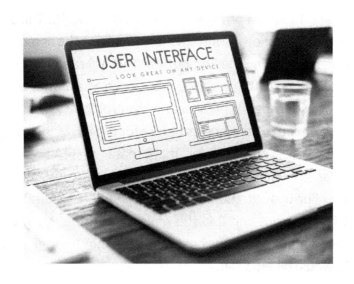

Arranging the system cards, also called system connectors, in Linux was previously a procedure that must be finished through the order line. This has changed as of late, and Kali Linux is the same. Kali Linux has a vigorous graphical UI (GUI) that enables a considerable lot of the basic settings to be designed using straightforward exchange boxes.

The system setups exchange box is effectively open by choosing Applications in the upper right of the UI and afterward choosing System Tools, Preferences, and Network associations. By clicking System associations, the System associations discourse box will be shown, and the Wired tab is chosen. On the other hand, right clicking on the two PCs on the upper right of the screen, and choosing Alter Associations will bring about getting to a similar exchange box. Much of the time, PCs will have just one system card that should be arranged, in situations where different NICs are introduced, guaranteeing you are designing the right card. This model will arrange Wired association 1, a name that can be changed if you like to use something increasingly significant, the main physical system card in the PC. The arrangement discourse box is shown subsequent to choosing the association with be changed and clicking the Edit button. This will raise the Editing box for the association, with the Wired tab chosen as a matter of course. This tab shows the gadget's media get to control (MAC) address, a location that is intended to continue as before for the life of the gadget (see the note on MAC addresses for more data on MAC addresses). The gadget's identifier is likewise shown in enclosure after the MAC address. For this situation, the gadget identifier is eth0, where eth is short for Ethernet and 0 is the main card in the PC. The numbering grouping for arrange cards begins at 0 and not 1 so the second card in the PC would be eth1.tab.

Wired Ethernet setups can be made by choosing the 802.1x Security tab, the IPv4 Settings, or the IPv6 Settings tab. This book will concentrate on designing the IP form 4 (IPv4) settings with the goal that tab will be chosen. When chosen the setups for the PCs IP address (192.168.1.66), Subnet Mask or Netmask (255.255.255.0), Gateway (192.168.1.1), and DNS servers (192.168.1.1). Various DNS servers can be utilized by isolating each with a comma. The arrangement can be spared and made dynamic by clicking the Save button.

Utilizing The Command Line to Configure Network Interfaces

It is critical to see how to arrange, or reconfigure, the system connector from the direction brief. This is valuable when not utilizing the graphical interface for Linux or in the event that you are associated with a framework remotely through a terminal window. There are various cases in entrance testing where the order line will be the main alternative for making setup changes.

These progressions should be made as a client with raised consents utilizing the root account. It is a decent method to roll out these improvements on a live conveyance and making them using the SDO direction is another alternative for establishments of Kali Linux. When consents have been raised, the system card can be arranged.

Checking the status of the PCs arrange cards and the status of each card is finished with the following order: ifconfig - a

This will show the present arrangement of all system cards on the PC. In Figure 4.7, two system addresses are shown, eth0, the principal Ethernet card and lo, the loopback or inner interface. The settings for this connector were set utilizing the graphical interface. Changing these is basic utilizing the direction brief.

Beginning and Stopping the Interface

The interface can be begun using the up choice or halted using the down choice of the ifconfig direction while indicating the interface to be halted or began. The accompanying direction would stop the main Ethernet connector.

The following order would begin the main Ethernet connector.

ifconfig eth0 up

The IP address of this connector can be changed from 192.168.1.66, its present arrangement, to 192.168.1.22 by utilizing the following direction.

ifconfig eth0 192.168.1.22

The order line can be utilized to change the system cover also by utilizing the accompanying direction. This will set the IP address to 192.168.1.22 and set the subnet veil to 255.255.0.0.

ifconfig eth0 192.168.1.22 netmask 255.255.255.0

Full arrangement of the system card at the direction line requires more work than utilizing the graphical UI as the setup settings are not all put away in a similar area. The default door is included or changed, for this situation to 192.168.1.2, with the accompanying direction.

Course include default gw 192.168.1.2

The name server (or DNS) settings are changed by altering the resolv.conf record in the /and so forth index. This can be changed by altering the record with your preferred proofreader or basically utilizing the accompanying order at the direction brief.

reverberation nameserver 4.4.4.4. /and so forth/resolv.conf

The above direction will evacuate the current nameserver and supplant it with 4.4.4.4. To include extra nameservers, the accompanying order will annex new nameserver addresses adding to those effectively recorded in resolv.conf.

At the point when the PC plays out a name query, it will check the initial three nameservers in the request they are recorded. reverberation nameserver 8.8.8.8. /and so on/resolv.conf

DHCP from the Command Prompt

Probably the most effortless approach to design a system card is to utilize DHCP administrations to arrange the card. Along these lines the DHCP server will supply the entirety of the setup settings required for the card. This is helpful for most end clients, however isn't ideal when leading entrance tests as the framework being arranged is signed in the

DHCP server's database. Utilize the following directions to incapacitate programmed DHCP setup when leading infiltration tests. This model uses the nano editorial manager; anyway other content tools can be utilized.

nano/and so on/organizing/interfaces

#add the accompanying lines##

auto eth0

iface eth0 inet static

address {IP_Address}

netmask {netmask}

passage {Gateway_IP_Address}

Spare the content document and exit to finish the adjustment. It might be necessary to bring down and bring back up the Ethernet interfaces to empower this arrangement.

To design the primary system card enter the following direction at the order brief.

dhclient eth0

This will consequently arrange the system card utilizing the settings gave by the DHCP server.

Utilizing The GUI to Configure Wireless Cards

Designing the remote system card can be practiced utilizing the GUI depicted earlier during the graphical setup of the Ethernet interface. For this situation, rather than choosing the tab for Wired, select the Wireless tab in the Network Connections exchange box.

From this tab select the Add button, which will show an exchange box titled "Altering Wireless association 1" (accepting this is the principal remote connector).

This discourse has four tabs that are used to empower setup of the remote card. This discourse box contains various settings that are utilized to design the framework's remote card.

Association Name

The association name setting defaults to "Remote association" followed by the quantity of the connector being arranged, for this situation Wireless association.

1. This name can be changed to something that is progressively significant, for example, customer 1 remote association.

Associate Automatically Checkbox

When the "Associate naturally" checkbox is chosen, the framework will consequently attempt to interface with the remote system when the PC is begun without client mediation. Like DHCP portrayed before, this might be helpful for most Linux clients. However, it is regularly not the best alternative for the infiltration analyzer as it might declare the analyzer's nearness on the system. If the checkbox is not selected, the analyzer will physically empower the remote connector.

Remote Tab Service Set Identifier

The administration set identifier (SSID) is the system name used to distinguish the remote system. Each system will have a solitary SSID that distinguishes the system, and this name will be utilized by customers to associate with the system. In systems with focal passageways, the SSID is determined to the passage and all customers must utilize that SSID to interface with the system. In systems with various passageways, the SSID must be the equivalent on each to empower correspondence.

Mode

The remote card can be designed in two modes either impromptu or foundation. Impromptu systems are regularly casual remote associations between PCs without a focal passageway performing the executive's capacities.

In these associations, every remote association must be arranged to coordinate each other PCs remote settings to set up the association. In foundation mode, focal passages deal with the customers associating with the system and to different PCs in the administration set. All customers must be designed to coordinate the settings characterized in the passageway. The fundamental contrast between these two alternatives is there is no focal organization in specially appointed systems administration while passageways midway oversee associations in framework mode.

Essential Service Set Identification

The essential assistance set identifier (BSSID) is utilized in framework mode to recognize the media to control (MAC) address of the passage. In contrast to the SSID, each passage will have a special BSSID as each ought to have a separate MAC address.

Gadget MAC Address

The field for the gadget MAC address is utilized to bolt this arrangement to a physical remote connector. This is advantageous when a PC has more than one remote connector. The drop down for this field will be populated with the MAC locations of remote dynamic connectors. Select the right MAC address for the connector you are designing.

Cloned MAC Address

Ordinarily the entrance analyzer won't have any desire to utilize the real MAC address of the connector that is being utilized on the PC. This might be done to sidestep straightforward security strategies, for example, MAC address sifting where just frameworks with explicit MAC delivers are permitted to associate with the system. This should likewise be possible to disguise your remote connector to seem, by all accounts, to be from another maker to coordinate those remote cards being utilized on the remote system.

Most Extreme Transmission Unit

The most extreme transmission unit (MTU) is a systems administration setting that is utilized to decide how huge the systems administration parcels can be to speak with the PC. Much of the time, the MTU can be set to programmed and will work fine. In situations where applications require a particular MTU, read that application's documentation to decide the MTU and set it here.

Remote Security Tab Security Drop Down

The Security drop-down zone is utilized to choose the strategy for verifying the remote system. For specially appointed systems, the system clients decide the right security settings, guaranteeing that every customer's security settings coordinate each other's PC in the system. In framework mode, every customer must be arranged to coordinate the security setting of the passageway.

Wired Equivalent Privacy

Wired Equivalent Privacy (WEP) is a more established security technique that utilizes essential encryption innovation to give security identical to wired frameworks. WEP utilizes either a 10 or 26 hexadecimal key to verify the correspondence. The WEP encryption standard has security imperfections that will permit infiltration analyzers to effectively break most WEP encryption keys. Dynamic WEP utilizes port safety efforts illuminated in IEEE 802.1x to give extra safety efforts to the remote system.

Lightweight Extensible Authentication Protocol

Lightweight Extensible Authentication Protocol (LEAP) was created by Cisco Systems to give improved security over the less secure WEP strategy. Jump is like Dynamic WEP.

Wi-Fi Protected Access

Wi-Fi Protected Access (WPA) is an entrance innovation that improves security of remote systems utilizing transient key respectability convention (TKIP) and trustworthiness checks. Systems utilizing WPA are substantially stronger to assaults than WEP-ensured remote systems. The underlying WPA standard was upgraded with the arrival of WPA2 by utilizing a more grounded security technique for encryption. In WPA-individual mode, every PC is designed utilizing a key created by a secret word or pass express. WPA undertaking requires a focal Remote Authentication Dial in User Service (RADIUS) server and 802.1x port safety efforts. While WPA venture is convoluted to set up, it gives extra safety efforts.

Passwords and Keys

On the off chance that WEP or WPA individual were chosen as the security technique starting from the drop, type the security key in the secret phrase/key field. Check the Show secret word/key checkbox to confirm the key being utilized has been composed effectively. In situations when the secret word ought not be shown, leave the checkbox unchecked. A few frameworks utilize a strategy for turning passwords or keys. If so, enter the secret word or key for each list by choosing the right list and afterward entering the right key or secret key for that file.

The system may have either open framework or shared key verification. In shared key verification, the passage sends a test instant message to the PC endeavoring to interface. The associating PC at that point scrambles the content with the WEP key and returns the encoded content to the passage.

The passage at that point permits the association if the encryption key utilized by the interfacing PC delivers the right encryption string. Open framework validation then again enables PCs to interface without this test and reaction arrangement, depending on the PC utilizing the right SSID. In the two cases, the correspondence channel is finished when the WEP key is utilized to verify the channel. While shared key verification may appear to be increasingly secure, it is in truth less secure as the test message and encoded content reaction are sent in clear content permitting anybody checking the remote channel to catch the test and reaction. As the WEP key is utilized to scramble the test, catching the test and reaction can permit the WEP key to be resolved.

Jump security utilizes the client name and secret word. These should be composed into the suitable fields when LEAP is chosen.

Dynamic WEP and WPA venture require various settings, endorsements, and designs to oversee. These settings won't be covered here; but, if you are joining a system that uses these techniques for security, essentially enter the right subtleties and give the right endorsements.

IPv4 Settings Tab

When the data in Wireless and Wireless Security tabs has been finished, the IPv4 arrangement can be finished. The procedure for designing these settings is the same as the procedure used to arrange the physical Ethernet association depicted earlier.

When the entirety of the necessary data has been given, save the settings by clicking the Save button. After the settings have been saved, the PC will attempt to interface with the system. This is imagined by a realistic in the upper right corner of the screen. Any mistakes will be shown in a discourse box.

Web Server

Kali Linux contains a simple-to-arrange Apache web server. Having an effectively configurable web server is a huge advantage to the entrance analyzer. For instance, utilizing this administration, sites can be made that copy existing pages on the Internet. These destinations would then be able to be utilized to serve malicious code to clients on the objective system. They will utilize social designing strategies like phishing, including assembling servers facilitating secondary passages, dealing with callbacks, and giving directions to different vindictive programming. There are various different uses the HTTP administration can be put to in an entrance test.

Utilizing the GUI to Start, Stop, or Restart the Apache Server

Utilizing the GUI is the most effortless approach to begin, stop, or restart/reset the web administration. To do this, select Applications from the bar at the highest point of the Kali screen. Starting from the drop down menu select Kali Linux, which will show a submenu. From this menu, select System Administrations, which will thus show another menu; select the HTTP choice on the fly-out menu. This will show the alternatives to begin, stop, and restart the Apache administration.

When a choice is produced using the menu, a direction shell will begin and the status of the server will be shown. Default establishments of Kali Linux will be shown when the Apache server is begun or restarted.

The blunder you may see is, "Couldn't dependably decide the server's completely qualified area name, utilizing 127.0.0.1 for ServerName." This mistake won't cause any issues now as the web server will be accessible on the system dependent on the framework's IP address. To address this mistake, alter the apache2.conf record in/and so forth/apache2/by adding the server name to be utilized after ServerName toward the finish of this document and afterward spare the record, as pursues.

ServerName localhost

At the point when the Apache server has been begun or restarted, the default site page can be reached by entering the PCs IP address in an internet browser. The Kali Linux circulation incorporates the IceWeasle internet browser that can be reached by clicking on the IceWeasle symbol on the top bar (a blue globe wrapped by a white weasel).

Beginning, Stopping, and Restarting Apache at the Command Prompt

The Apache HTTP server can be effectively begun, halted, and restarted utilizing the order/and so on/init.d/apache2 followed by the activity mentioned (stop, start, or restart). Utilizing the order line brings about indistinguishable activities from the GUI.

/and so on/init.d/apache2 start

/and so forth/init.d/apache2 stop

/and so forth/init.d/apache2 restart

The Default Web Page

When the Apache administration is ready for action the default (It works!) site page should be changed. To do this, make the web content that ought to be shown on the page and spare it as index.html in the/var/www/catalog. Then again, the current index.html document at this area can be altered and new pages can be included.

FTP Server

The File Transfer Protocol (FTP) is utilized to move documents between PCs. Note that FTP doesn't encode documents or the correspondence channel between PCs so any record navigating the system (or Internet) between the PCs can be seen by anybody observing the system.

Kali Linux does exclude an FTP server so one can be added to encourage moving documents between frameworks. There are various FTP benefits that can be included, one of these is the Pure-FTPd (http://www.pureftpd.org/venture/unadulterated ftpd); notwithstanding, any bolstered FTP daemon ought to be worthy.

Utilize the adept get direction to download and introduce the Pure-FTPd administration using the following order. adept get introduce unadulterated ftpd-basic unadulterated ftpd

This will introduce and set up the FTP administration. Some minor setup is important to guarantee appropriate activity of the Pure-FTP Server.

compact disc/and so forth/unadulterated ftpd/conf

reverberation no. Tie

reverberation no. PAMAuthentication

reverberation no. UnixAuthentication

In - s/and so on/unadulterated ftpd/conf/PureDB/and so forth/unadulterated ftpd/auth/50pure

Next gatherings and clients for the FTP administration must be made. First make another framework gathering.

Next include the recently made gathering. This order will give the client no consent to the home index or shell get to.

useradd g ftpgroup - d/dev/invalid s/receptacle/bogus ftpuser

Make a registry for ftp records.

mkdir - p/home/pubftp

Add client envelopes to the ftp registry. For this situation, the client sam that will be made needs an index.

mkdir /home/pubftp/sam

Now include a client and secret word for the FTP administration. For this situation, the client sam is made.

unadulterated pw useradd sam u ftpuser g ftpgroup d /home/pubftp/sam

A brief will require a secret word be made.

Utilize the following order to refresh the Pure-FTPd database.

unadulterated pw mkdb

At last start the FTP administration with the accompanying direction.

administration unadulterated ftpd start

In the wake of beginning Pure-FTPd, it's a smart thought to test it utilizing the accompanying direction.

ftp {IP_Address}

When indicated enter client name sam and secret phrase. If confirmation was fruitful, the FTP server is working effectively. If this was not effective, reboot the PC and attempt to ftp to the server once more.

The guide from http://samiux.blogspot.com/2011/08/howto-unadulterated ftpd-andatftpd-on-backtrack.html was utilized to finish the important strides to make Pure-FTPd practical.

SSH Server

Secure Shell (SSH) is a progressively secure technique for getting to the substance of the Kali Linux record framework from remote areas. SSH gives a protected, encoded interchanges channel between the conveying PCs.

This is useful for infiltration analyzers as it permits record moves to happen without being investigated by organize security devices like interruption identification framework (IDS) and interruption counteractive action framework (IPS).

Produce SSH Keys

To safely utilize SSH, encryption keys must be produced to encourage secure and encoded correspondence. To produce these keys, enter the following at the order brief.

Move the first SSH keys from their default index; don't erase them.

mkdir - p/and so on/ssh/original_keys

mv/and so on/ssh/ssh_host_*/and so on/ssh/original_keys

compact disc/and so on/ssh

Create new SSH keys.

dpkg-reconfigure openssh-server

Start/restart the SSH Daemon.

administration ssh (start j restart)

Dealing with the SSH Service from the Kali GUI

The SSH server is incorporated with the primary document structure of the Kali GUI and is gotten to in a similar way that the Apache server is begun or halted. To get to the SSH menu, select Applications from the bar at the highest point of the Kali screen. From the drop down menu that is displayed select Kali Linux. Then select System Services; from the next menu, select the SSH choice on SSH Server 55 the fly-out menu. This will show the choices to begin, stop, and restart the SSH administration.

Dealing with the SSH Server from the Command Line The SSH server can be begun, halted and restarted from here also. Do this after the direction/and so on/init.d/ssh, as outlined in the following directions.

/and so forth/init.d/ssh start

/and so on/init.d/ssh stop

/and so on/init.d/ssh restart

Getting to the Remote System

When the SSH administration is begun on the Kali framework, the PC can be accessed remotely from Linux frameworks by entering the following direction at the order brief (with a client name of sam and a remote framework IP address of 192.168.1.66).

ssh sam@192.168.1.66

Getting to SSH from a Windows customer will require the utilization of a SSH customer.

A significant number of these are accessible in the Internet; for instance putty is a generally utilized instrument that is accessible from http://putty.org. Introduce the customer and give the IP address or name of the Kali Linux PC as sign in certifications and interface with the remote Kali PC.

Design And Access External Media

Getting to outer media like hard drives or thumb drives is a lot simpler in Kali Linux than in prior adaptations of Backtrack. By and large, media associated with the framework utilizing an all-inclusive sequential transport (USB) connector will be identified and made accessible by the working framework. Nonetheless, if this doesn't occur consequently, physically mounting the drive might be necessary.

Physically Mounting a Drive

The primary thing that must be done when physically mounting a drive to Kali Linux is to interface the physical drive to the PC. Next open an order incite and make a mount point. To make the mount point consents for the record being utilized should be raised; this should be possible with the sudo order if the root account isn't being utilized. The accompanying order will make a mount point called newdrive in the media index.

Decide the drive and segment you are interfacing utilizing the fdisk direction with subtleties on the drive you are appending. The primary hard drive will ordinarily be hda, and the main segment on this drive will be hda1. This arrangement proceeds with extra drives associated with the PC with the second being hdb and the third being hdc. More often than not, the essential inside drive will be marked hda so the principal outside drive will be named hdb. To mount the main segment of hdb to the newdrive index made in the last advance use the following order.

mount/dev/hdb1/media/newdrive

When this is finished, the substance of the drive will be accessible by exploring the newdrive index.

compact disc/media/newdrive

Refreshing Kali

Like other working frameworks, Kali has the worked in capacity to refresh both the working framework and the applications, or bundles, introduced. As updates to bundles become accessible, they will be presented on the Kali store. This archive could then be checked to guarantee the working framework and applications are cutting-edge. Updates are ordinarily smaller fixes that address programming bugs, or mistakes, or are utilized to include new equipment capacities. Refreshing Kali should be possible with the adept get order line utility. able get update

Redesigning Kali

Like refreshing, redesigning Kali should also be possible at the direction line with the able get utility. Overhauls are ordinarily significant amendments to applications or the working framework itself. Overhauls offer new usefulness and are a lot bigger than updates typically requiring additional existence on the frameworks drive - able get overhaul

CPSIA information can be obtained
at www.ICGtesting.com
Printed in the USA
LVHW021720090521
686930LV00013B/910